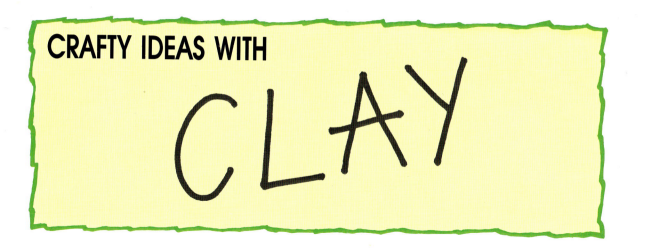

CRAFTY IDEAS WITH CLAY

Melanie Rice

Illustrated by Lynne Farmer

Photography by Chris Fairclough

HODDER AND STOUGHTON
LONDON   SYDNEY   AUCKLAND   TORONTO

To Chris, Catherine and Alex, for all their help.

British Library Cataloguing in Publication Data
Rice, Melanie
 Crafty ideas with clay.
 1. Modelling in clay. For children
 I. Title
 731.4′2
 ISBN 0-340-50109-X

Text copyright © Melanie Rice 1989
Illustrations copyright © Lynne Farmer 1989

First published 1989

All rights reserved. No part of this publication may be reproduced or transmitted in any form or by any means, electronically or mechanically, including photocopying, recording, or any information storage and retrieval system, without either prior permission in writing from the publisher or a licence permitting restricted copying. In the United Kingdom such licences are issued by the Copyright Licensing Agency, 33-34 Alfred Place, London WC1E 7DP.

Published by Hodder and Stoughton Children's Books, a division of Hodder and Stoughton Ltd, Mill Road, Dunton Green, Sevenoaks, Kent TN13 2YA

Design by Sally Boothroyd

Cover illustration by Lynn Breeze

Book list compiled by Peter Bone, Senior Librarian, Children's and Schools Services, Hampshire County Library

Printed in Italy

CONTENTS

	Page
Notes to readers	4
Wind chimes	6
Drum	8
Christmas night-light	10
Finger puppets	12
Pendants	14
Solitaire	16
Dinosaurs	18
Hedgehog desk tidy	20
Froggy-bank	22
Wall plaque	24
Flowerpot-holder	26
Soap-holder	28
Book list	30
Index	31

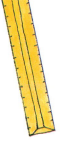

Note to parents and teachers

All the ideas in this book are easy to carry out at home or at school. Every item has been made by my own young children and then photographed for this book. Each page has clear instructions accompanied by numbered, easy-to-follow illustrations.

Self-hardening clay has been used throughout so there is no need for a kiln to fire the finished objects. Clay of this type can be painted with watercolour paints and coated in an ordinary acrylic varnish. You can either buy your own tools or, to save expense, make use of old kitchen utensils and other things lying around the home – for example, a rolling pin, knife, nail and knitting needle. Stand the clay objects on a wire rack, or something similar, for a day or two while they harden.

Pieces of clay are joined together using SLIP – a special glue made from clay itself. To make slip, place a small amount of clay in a pot and mix with water until it resembles thick cream.

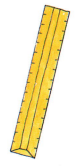

Note to children

Things to remember:

1 Read all the instructions carefully before you begin so that you know what you have to do. Use the illustrations to help you.

2 Make sure everything you need is ready before you start.

3 Spread newspaper over your working surface – this is especially important for messy projects.

4 Clean up any mess when you have finished.

5 Put everything away tidily.

At the end of each project I have suggested other things for you to make. Maybe you have some ideas of your own. Don't be afraid to try them out.

Melanie Rice

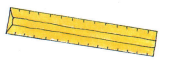

WIND CHIMES

Hang these wind chimes by a door or open window and listen to the wind blowing through them.

You will need:

clay
a knitting needle
paint
sponge
varnish
water

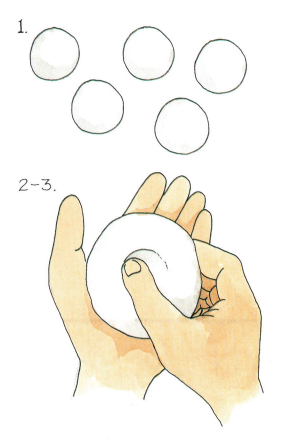

1 Roll six small balls of clay.

2 Press your thumb into the middle of a ball and squeeze between thumb and fingers.

3 Turn the clay in the palm of your cupped hand, squeezing the sides so they become thinner.

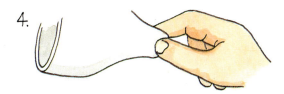
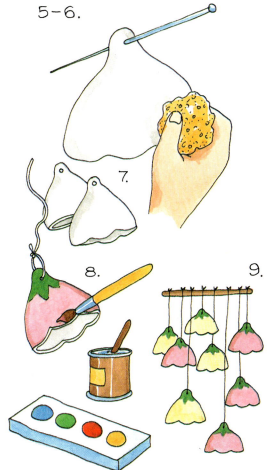

4 Pinch the bottom to make a stem.

5 Make a hole through the stem with a knitting needle.

6 Smooth the surface with a damp sponge.

7 Now do the same with the other lumps of clay.

8 Leave to harden, then paint and varnish.

9 Attach a thread to each stem and hang from a stick.

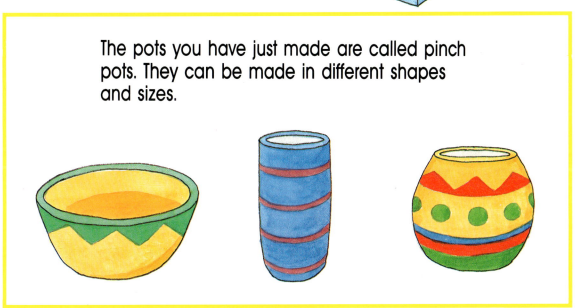

The pots you have just made are called pinch pots. They can be made in different shapes and sizes.

DRUM

Make your own African drum like this one. Paint it using strong bright colours and patterns.

You will need:

clay
elastic band
greaseproof paper
paint
scissors
slip and brush
sponge
varnish
water

1 Roll some clay into a ball.

2 Press both thumbs into the middle and squeeze between thumbs and fingers.

3 Turn the pot and continue squeezing. Try to make the sides the same thickness all round.

4 When the pot is shaped like a bowl, brush some slip round the top edge.

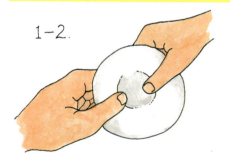

5 Take some more clay and roll into a sausage shape. Curl round the edge of the pot and press down firmly.

6 Smooth with a damp sponge.

7 Leave to harden, then paint and varnish.

8 Cut out a circle of greaseproof paper and place over the top. Secure with elastic band.

A 'shaker' is another percussion instrument you can make from pinch pots.

Make two pinch pots. Fill one with split peas then join them with slip. Push a stick into one end as a handle. Shake.

CHRISTMAS NIGHT-LIGHT

This candle-holder was made with Christmas in mind, but you can substitute other shapes for the fir trees to make it useful all year round.

You will need:

cardboard
clay
knife
paint
pastry cutter
pencil
rolling pin
ruler
scissors
slip and brush
sponge
sticky tape
varnish
water

1 Cut out five squares of card (8cm × 8cm each). Use them as a template to cut five squares of clay.

2 Join the pieces of card with sticky tape to make a box, as shown, and put one of the squares of clay into the bottom of the box.

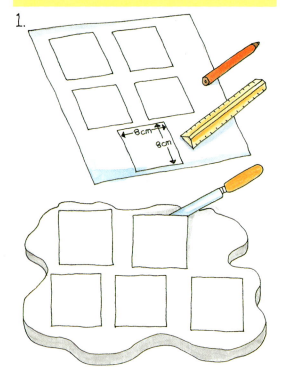

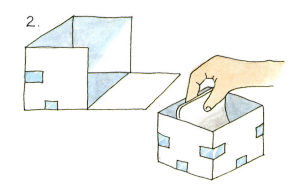

3 Cut out a tree shape from each of the other four pieces of clay. Now stick each tree back onto its square alongside the tree-shaped hole. Press down firmly.

4 Paste slip round the edges of the clay base inside the box and stick one clay square to the base, inside the card, as a wall piece (with the pattern side towards the card). Paste slip to the edges of this piece.

5 Put the other three clay squares into the box in the same way to make the other three sides.

6 Press the joins firmly together. Roll four sausages of clay and stick them inside the joins, as shown, to strengthen them.

7 Leave to harden. Remove the card, then paint and varnish.

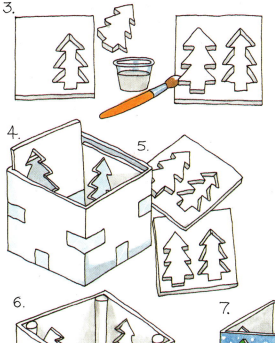

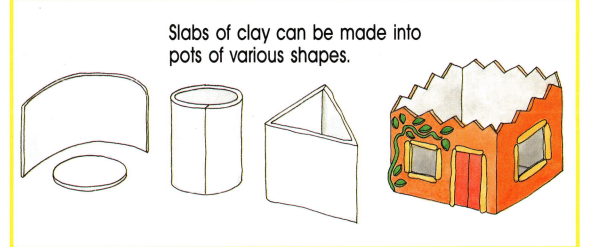

Slabs of clay can be made into pots of various shapes.

FINGER PUPPETS

The angry-looking heads on these finger puppets are ideal for acting out plays.

You will need:

clay
paint
pencil
slip and brush
varnish
water

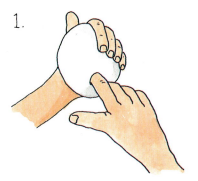

1. Roll a ball of clay. Push your index finger into the middle.

2. Squeeze the sides gently with your other hand.

3. Pull some of the clay forward to shape it into a nose as shown. Make hair either by drawing pieces out from the top, or by scratching lines on the surface with the point of a pencil.

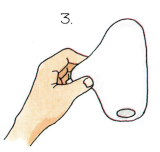
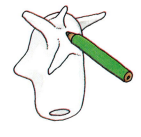

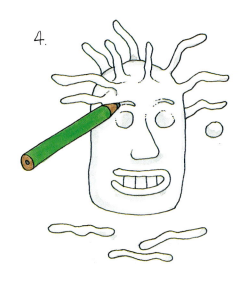

4 Scratch in eyebrows using the pencil. Make holes for the eyes. Roll two small balls of clay and stick into eye sockets. Roll a sausage of clay and stick it on to make the mouth.

5 Leave to harden, then paint and varnish.

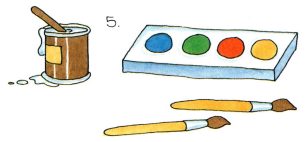

You can stick or tie material to the heads to make a variety of interesting characters.

PENDANTS

Find a use for broken brooches and necklaces, odd sequins or spare buttons by making them into sparkling new jewellery.

You will need:

clay
knitting needle
paint
pastry cutter or knife
rolling pin
sequins, beads, buttons,
   paste jewels
sponge
varnish
water

1 Roll out a slab of clay, about 1cm thick.

2 Using a knife or pastry cutter, cut out the shapes you want. Smooth the edges with a damp sponge.

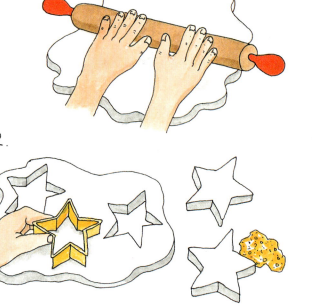

14

3.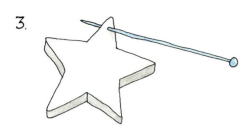

4.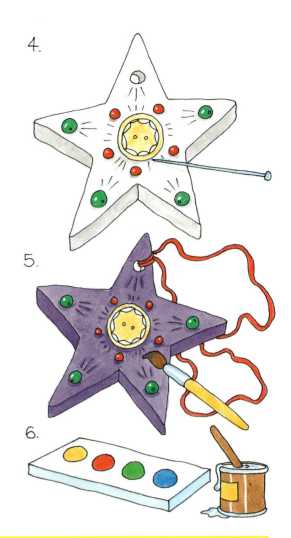

3 Make a hole through the top with the knitting needle.

4 Press buttons, beads, sequins or jewels into the clay. Using a knife or the point of a knitting needle, scratch sun rays round the jewels as shown.

5 Leave to harden. The decorations should now be firmly in place because clay shrinks as it dries. If they loosen, stick them back with a dab of glue.

6 Paint and varnish.

More jewellery.

You can make a brooch in the same way, but press a safety pin into the back before the clay hardens.

To make earrings, thread a loop of wire through the hole at the top as shown. Attach to an earring clip.

15

SOLITAIRE

This game is easy to make and can be played alone or with a friend. Decorate the board and marbles in any style you like to make your own personal set.

You will need:

clay
marble
paint
rolling pin
sponge
varnish
water

1 Roll out a slab of clay, about 2cm thick.

2 Cut out a large circle – use a dinner plate or something similar to guide you.

3 Dent the clay with a marble. Follow the pattern shown.

4 Smooth the surface with a damp sponge.

5 Make a clay marble by rolling a small piece of clay in the palms of your hands. Do this another thirty-two times!

6 Leave to harden, then paint and varnish. One marble should be a different colour from the rest.

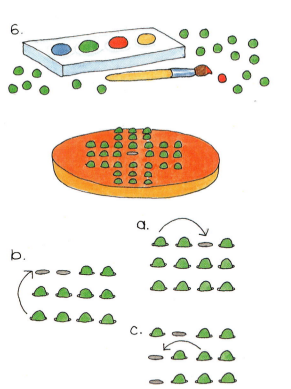

To play solitaire

Place the marbles on the board, leaving the centre hole empty. A marble moves by jumping backwards, or forwards, or sideways over another marble into an empty hole. The marble that is jumped over is then taken away. The aim is to remove all the marbles from the board in this way, until only one remains.

Fox and Geese (a game to play with a friend).

Lay out fourteen marbles as shown – one fox and thirteen geese.

The geese can move one hole at a time in any direction. The fox can move only if he can jump over a goose and land in an empty hole. He then removes the goose from the board. The geese must try to hem the fox in so that he cannot move.

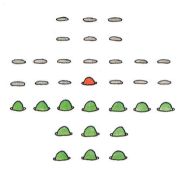

A fox may catch two geese at a time

DINOSAURS

Dinosaurs are easy to make and are cheaper to keep than pets!

You will need:

clay
nail
paint
slip and brush
varnish
water

1 Roll a sausage of clay, thicker in the middle than at the ends.

2 Shape one end to make a head as shown and pinch the other to make a pointed tail.

3 Roll four thick sausages for the legs and stick them to the body with slip.

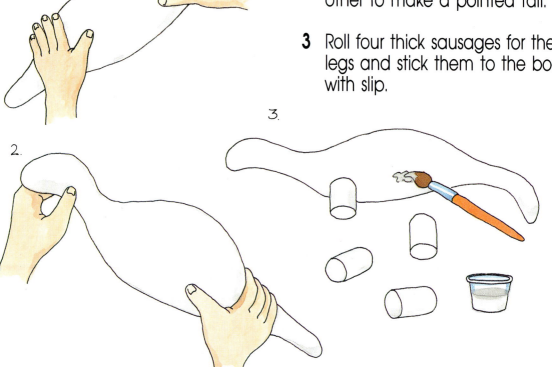

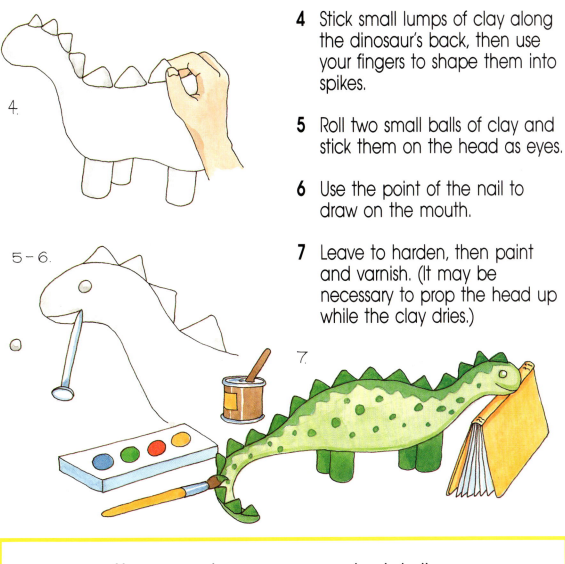

4 Stick small lumps of clay along the dinosaur's back, then use your fingers to shape them into spikes.

5 Roll two small balls of clay and stick them on the head as eyes.

6 Use the point of the nail to draw on the mouth.

7 Leave to harden, then paint and varnish. (It may be necessary to prop the head up while the clay dries.)

You can make many more animals in the same way. Here are some examples. I am sure you can think of your own.

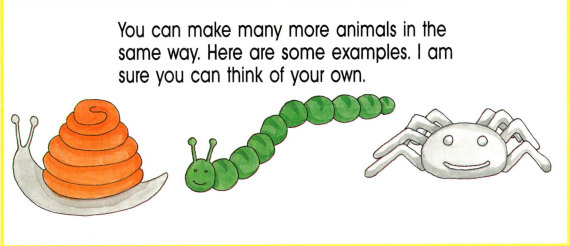

HEDGEHOG DESK TIDY

Make yourself this hedgehog desk tidy and you will never have to look for your pens and pencils again.

You will need:

clay
knife
paint
pencil
rolling pin
slip and brush
varnish
water

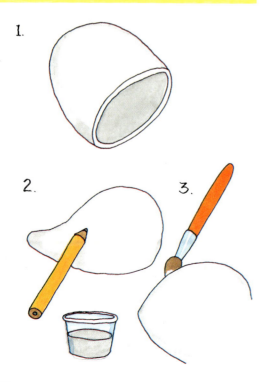

1 Roll some clay into a ball and make a pinch pot with sides 1cm thick.

2 Now roll another ball of clay and shape it to make the head and nose as shown. Use the point of a pencil to draw two eyes.

3 Stick the head to the body using slip.

4 Make holes through the body with a pencil, then scratch on 'prickles' using the pencil point.

5 Leave to dry.

6 Roll out a slab of clay to make the base. Place the hedgehog on top and cut round the outline with a knife.

7 Roll a thin sausage of clay and stick it to the edge of the base as shown.

8 Leave to harden, then paint and varnish.

You may think of other shapes for a desk tidy. Here are some ideas.

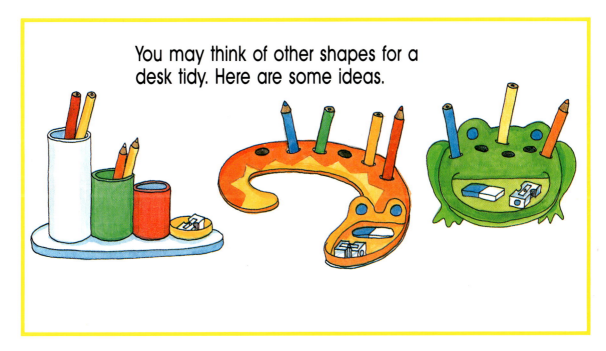

FROGGY-BANK

You can use your frog to look after your holiday savings, or put him on a shelf as an ornament.

You will need:

clay
knife
paint
rolling pin
slip and brush
sponge
varnish
water

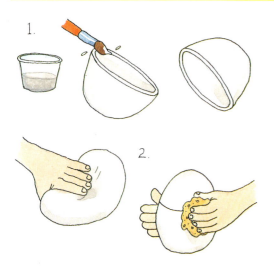

1 Make two pinch pots. Join them using slip.

2 Smooth the surface with a damp sponge.

3 Roll a ball of clay and shape it to make the frog's head as shown. Build up the eyes by adding small pieces of clay, stuck down with slip.

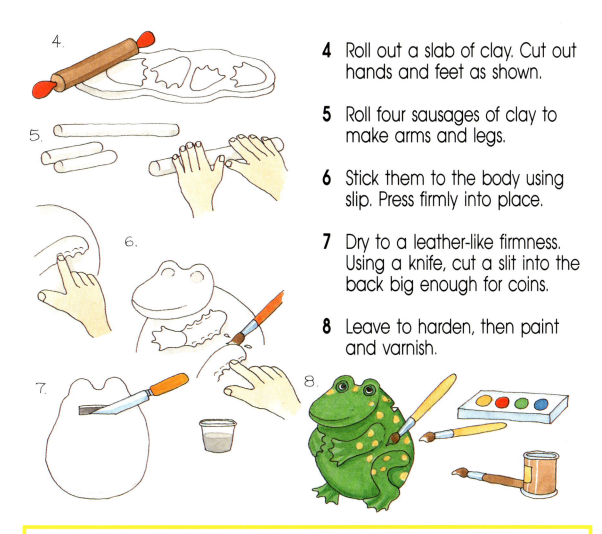

4 Roll out a slab of clay. Cut out hands and feet as shown.

5 Roll four sausages of clay to make arms and legs.

6 Stick them to the body using slip. Press firmly into place.

7 Dry to a leather-like firmness. Using a knife, cut a slit into the back big enough for coins.

8 Leave to harden, then paint and varnish.

Two pinch pots joined can be used to make other animal shapes.

WALL PLAQUE

This picture will make a beautiful present. It can be made with designs specially chosen to suit the person it is for.

You will need:

clay
knife
paint
pencil
rolling pin
slip and brush
sponge
varnish
water

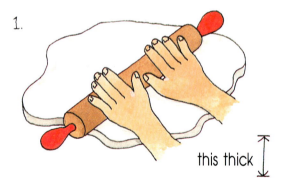

this thick

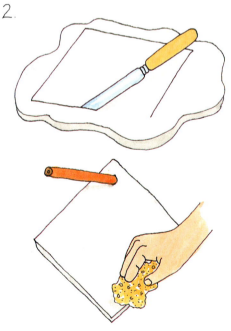

1 Roll out a slab of clay 1cm thick.

2 Cut the sides to make a square. Make a hole in one corner to hang it up by and smooth the edges with a damp sponge.

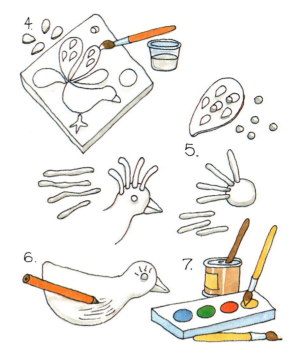

3 Roll another slab of clay and cut out the shapes as shown.

4 Stick the largest shapes (marked 'a') into place using slip, then add the smaller ones ('b').

5 Roll some small balls of clay to decorate the feathers and to make an eye. Roll sausages to make the plume and the rays of the sun. Stick everything into place, pressing down gently but firmly.

6 Scratch feather patterns on to the wings with the point of a pencil.

7 Leave to harden, then paint and varnish.

You can make other pictures using different shapes (choose colourful subjects).

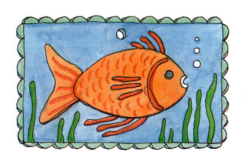

FLOWERPOT-HOLDER

The pot-holder is called a coil pot because it is made by piling up coils of clay. People have been making pots this way for thousands of years.

You will need:

card (to use as a scraper)
clay
knife
paint
rolling pin
slip and brush
sponge
varnish
water

1.

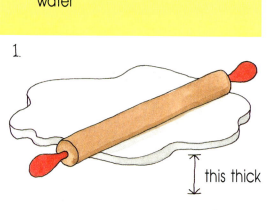

this thick

1 Roll out a slab of clay about 1cm thick. Cut round something circular to make the base.

2 Roll a sausage or coil of clay about 1cm in diameter and stick to the base with slip.

2.

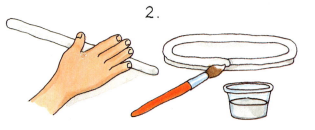

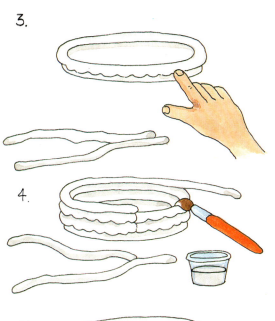

3 Join the coil to the base by pressing as shown.

4 Make another 7 coils in the same way and build them one on top of the other. Stick each with slip and press down on the coil below.

5 Scrape the outside of the pot with a card scraper to remove any bumps, then smooth the surface with a damp sponge.

6 Leave to harden, then paint and varnish.

Coil pots can be made in many shapes and sizes. Try making the coils a little longer each time – or a little shorter.

SOAP-HOLDER

Keep your soap-holder to brighten up your own bathroom, or give it to a friend as a present.

You will need:

clay
damp cloth
knife
small margarine tub
paint
pencil
sponge
slip and brush
varnish
water

1 Cover the margarine tub with a damp cloth.

2 Roll out a circular slab of clay and lay it over the upturned tub.

3 Trim the extra clay from the base and squeeze the folds of clay together at either side. One side will become the tail, the other the neck.

4 Roll out another slab of clay and cut out two wings and a crest as shown.

5 Roll a ball to make the head. Pull some clay forward and shape into a beak. Roll two small balls of clay for the eyes and stick them to the head with slip.

6 When the body is firm to the touch, remove it gently from the margarine tub and stick on the wings, head and crest as shown.

7 Smooth all the edges with a sponge.

8 Using the pencil, scratch feather patterns on the wings and tail.

9 Leave to harden, then paint and varnish.

You can use other objects instead of the margarine tub to mould the clay into interesting shapes.

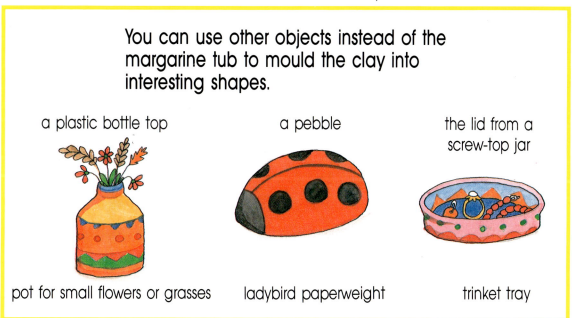

a plastic bottle top — pot for small flowers or grasses

a pebble — ladybird paperweight

the lid from a screw-top jar — trinket tray

29

BOOK LIST

If you want more ideas for practical craft activities the following books may be of interest. Your local library should be able to get copies for you.

Coleman, Anne.
FABRICS AND YARNS
Wayland, 1989. 1852106743
A book from the 'Craft Projects' series which has step by step drawings to show how materials can be used for a range of imaginative projects.

Devonshire, Hilary.
COLLAGE
Franklin Watts, 1988. 0863137091
A range of collage ideas which includes use of cork, sand, wool, fabric and paper. Also gives some ideas on how to mix these materials in one picture.

Hart, Tony.
MAKING TREASURE
Kaye & Ward, 1983. 071822955X
The most simple of craft books showing how to make gold coins, jewellery and a treasure chest; all from household materials. A slim volume with simple ideas.

Lancaster, John.
CARD
Franklin Watts, 1989. 0863138063
A lavishly illustrated book with some intricate sculptures. Helpful sections on scoring and bending card.

Pitcher, Caroline.
ANIMALS
Franklin Watts, 1983. 0863130437
How to make cows, snakes, dogs, hedgehogs and many more creatures, from things that are found in most homes and classrooms. Instructions for the projects are given by illustrations and there is not much written description.

Roussel, Mike.
CLAY
Wayland, 1989. 185210533X
A well-illustrated book on clay modelling with simple instructions covering various techniques from solid shaped models to pinch pots and coiling.

For older children

Curtis, Annabelle, and Hindley, Judy.
THE KNOW HOW BOOK OF PAPER FUN
Usborne, 1975. 0860200000
A successful collection of things to make from paper and card in which the easiest ideas are at the beginning. It covers pop-up cards and mobiles as well as the more complex crocodile marionettes and a Jack-in-the-box.

Potter, Tony.
POTTERY
Usborne, 1985. 0860209458
A book which gives some detail about how clay can be used, but which does not necessarily involve much equipment. Plenty of ideas for a multitude of projects.

INDEX

animals 18, 19, 20, 21, 22, 23

beads 14, 15
brooches 14, 15
buttons 14, 15

candle-holder 10–11
coil pot 26, 27

desk tidy 20–21
dinosaurs 18–19
drum 8–9

earrings 15

flowerpot-holder 26–27
froggy-bank 22–23

game 16–17

necklaces 14, 15

paperweight 29
pendants 14–15
pinch pots 6, 7, 8, 9, 22, 23
puppets 12–13

sequins 14, 15
shaker 9
slab pots 10, 11
soap-holder 28–29

trinket tray 29

wall plaque 24–25
wind chimes 6–7